Watershed

Watershed

Poems by

Rae Spencer

Cover design by Shay Culligan

ISBN: 978-1-63980-389-7

Kelsay Books
502 South 1040 East, A-119
American Fork, Utah 84003
Kelsaybooks.com

Dedicated to the Albright Poets and to the mermaids.
Without them, I would have no words.

Acknowledgments

I would like to thank the editors, poets, and readers who make time in their lives for poetry, with special thanks to the venues that first published poems in this collection.

Autumn Sky Poetry DAILY: "The Fire, Part I"
Blue Hour: "Another Autumn"
Bolts of Silk: "Of Warbler and Quail," "Finalizing Our Aged Property"
Contemporary American Voices: "Spell Out a Robin, for Cheer," "In the Suburbs, Night Rises"
Foundling Review: "Longing"
Grey Sparrow Journal: "A Dove, for Beginnings," "Rescue"
Liberal Arts & Education: "Poet's Block"
Melusine, or Woman in the 21ˢᵗ Century: "Daphne in the Spring"
The Orange Room Review: "A Jay, for Quarrelsome Lines"
Poetry Breakfast: "Metamorphosis"
Rose & Thorn Journal: "Where I Once Belonged"
Sliver of Stone: "Autumn"
Steam Ticket: "The Bowerbird's Courtship"
Triggerfish Critical Review: "The Burn"
vox poetica: "Gravity," "After the Birthday," "The Tracking," "Entropy," "Doppler Effect"
Willows Wept Review: "Waking"
Your Daily Poem: "The Dive," "Separating the Irises"

Contents

Part Three: Rain Water

Coda

The Dive

What is splash to the spectator
Elegant rip and lovely arc
And the hiss of bubbles rising

Is roar to the diver
Violent crash and sudden dark
The chaos of an unloving element
And the marvelous
Lyrical strain of body
Asserting its right of entry

The audience sees flight
Instead of gravity
The illusion of grace

In the tendon-taut
Wrench of the dive
All muscle and form
Bone and breath and certainty
The goal is met
Not in air

But in water
Where the diver's mass
No longer discerns

Some divers have been lost
Have pushed deeper and deeper
Their affinity for surface
Confused
Though, given rein
Their flesh might have risen

Buoyed by its lighter resin
Which aches
To emerge

Sated and weary
Bone-drenched
In true grace
The gleaming self
May seem ungainly
After such a glorious fall

That lasted but a breath
Lovely arc and elegant rip
And the hiss of bubbles rising

Part One
Ground Water

The Fire, Part I

In the house of my youth we burned
Wood for warmth, cut cords of kindling
Or bought from the neighbor tumbled
Ricks, split and ready to stack in the shed

We brought the fire indoors, caged
In a cave of brick and iron where it paced
From log to log in restless ember
Bright crackle damped in the stove

To slow radiant glow, though some nights
Wind turned right and flame rushed
The chimney with a rumbled roar
Raced on swirling drafts until resin ran

In audible runnel through the creaking pipe
Dammed the elbow bend, which we cleaned
By hand after starving the feral flare
Choking its breath into cold char

Dumped on the mound to be whittled
By gust and rain while we learned
To feed our flame a gentler timber
Avoiding hickory's hot heart, which raged

In the stove, warping flange and grate
While summer-felled oak, cured for a season
Soothed softer heat through that lazy
Room, the paneled den of books and sleep

Dogs sprawled in a row before the stove
Cats weaving past the door to bask
Between hunts, between journeys afield
To measure the world and mark their place

With scent and claw before returning home
Fur soaked with smoke, like our clothes
And rugs, shelves and stories, everything
Touched by the fire we kept inside

The Farm Daughters

We cherished all the strays
all the scrawny toms and pregnant queens
the cowering welted dogs
and puppies thrown from cars
the herds of clumsy ducks
speckled chicks and guinea fowl
our scruffy brush-fed goats

One spring we rescued tadpoles
from the pond's leaking mire
a trio of angels in muddy brigade
eager for the magic
of metamorphosis
but the ducks, mistaking our intentions
feasted overnight

Cruel with curiosity
we cast crickets into webs
to prompt the writing spiders
to see the pounce and bite and damp cocoon
spooled in morning dew
like silken memories

of lightning bugs in mason jars
the scent of wasted pheromones
and the snakes our father feared

He vented Adam's rage in swerving tires
and shovel blades and bullets
Undeterred, rat snakes stole the chickens' eggs
and, after our father left,
king snakes ate the vipers in our garden

Adaptation

Some days I hardly remember
what it is to fly

what loss is
When morning feels like betrayal
and shoulders ache
with the sudden load of gravity
pressed into cruel bones
too human for wings

As if I never once awoke
hair smelling of clouds
wound in wild knots
and damp with tears

or slept
curled in a crevice of wind

Other days I recall myself
grace confined to memory
in which I have never flown
and it was only ever a tale
from childhood
I was never meant to believe

Longing

How would I know age
If youth had not come first
If I never loved my mother's hands
Her graceful Itsy Bitsy Spider
Whirling on the waterspout
How would I cherish
My own tendons and lines

Would I know need
If I never read Lassie Come Home
Or yearned for feelings I couldn't hold
Cried for a sadness that might have been anger
Or grief
Or simply a puppy
I couldn't name and keep

Would my thirties know sorrow and loss
And regret
If my teens didn't know them first
If I never found my private brook
And memorized its every curve
And thought myself the only girl
To ever walk its banks
Would age be like stepping into water
Barely sensate
Unaware of how I once
Leapt far from the bank
Without needing to know
What depths would find me

Would age come at all
If youth didn't long for it
Search for ways to hurry it

For the simple freedom
Of knowing grief from anger
And choosing what things
To name and keep

Like the memory of my mother's hands
Trying to explain
The nature of longing
How I would always be

That Itsy Bitsy Spider
Yearning for whatever waits
Atop the waterspout

A Jay, for Quarrelsome Lines

Blue-barred beauty
Loud and brash
They nested over the clothesline
Pulled hair while I worked

While I hurried, yanking hard
So wooden-spring pins
Splattered from sheets
Soaked in a stormy wind

Mother scolded
Because I was too late
Or too lazy
And the towels mildewed

From being folded damp
Rain-sweet and stiff

The jays harassed our cats
Our beagle dogs
Chained beneath the tree
Our neighbors' cats and dogs

And all the other birds
Who knew only song
Only the twitter of seed
From sunflower, heavy with oil

Bowed beneath the weight of summer
Which baked everything brown
Except the blue-barred jays
Heat sapped everything weak

Everything except the jays, who raised
Their quarrelsome brood above the clothesline

Watershed

Really just a stream
What we called simply
"Creek" (in accent: "crick")
Shallow rills for summer wading
Cold flanks of limestone spring

We ragged group of nymphs
Sisters of my youth
Bolted gaily, daily
Down the hills, pooled
Ourselves beside the bank

We harried crawdads from their dens
Gave silver minnows fairy names
We saw ourselves in damselflies
Molting toward our adult wings
Sustained by infant gills

What snakes we found in Eden
We kept all summer in our rooms
Their flicking tongues, feather light
Spoke nothing of temptation
We loosed them in the fall

As time loosed us one season
To gain the winnowed air
We gleamed in bright emergence
Damp jewels ferried on a breeze
Into brilliant scattered flight

After the Birthday

Remember when you sometimes got
Exactly what you wanted
And it *was* what you wanted?

Remember when the things you wanted
Were gettable? And real?

Remember six? Or nine?

Never at twelve, never at anything teen
Twenty happened to discover
How wanting made the getting better
And less likely

Then thirty realized wanting
Was another form of leisure
A luxury for the young

Who sometimes got exactly
What they wanted, and knew

Want was all they needed

Enough want, enough true want
Innocent and pure, hard and honest
Wishes and prayers and tears
The knotted path of relentless
Scheme and plots, for that one thing

The only thing you wanted, ever
And sometimes it came
In a box or a bag, tromping
Through the frosted door

On some special day
With candles and lights and joy
When the knot slipped loose

In magician hands, and you got
Exactly what you wanted

And you would never want again

The Burn

Who could remember the scald?
Too small, too young
Too infant for remembrance

Four older siblings recall
Four different parts of the tale
Our Mother remembers it all

My memory starts with the scar
Sprawled across my foot
Tentacle deep in tissue
Nerve beyond any sensation
Everything prone to sunburn

It could almost be a joke
If it had ever been funny
For any of us

For any at the supper table
Who witnessed how long
My infant arms would reach

It could almost be a joke
To be forever marked
By pot-pie
Deep and deep and deep
The burn scarred skin and more

A tendon, thick and pulled
Right foot duck, left foot not
And Mother fought that turn

"Straighten your foot . . .
You can make it right
when you want."

Which I could
So she never understood
As mothers and daughters never do
In the heat of nest-leaving
We never understood

Why I tolerated my awkward turn
Why I let my scar, or any burn
Pull in a direction

That angled away
From everything
She saw in me

Waking

At seventeen I knew I'd die
A shared intuition
Among my peers
If only I had known

That every friend and foe
Would arrive, like me
Ill prepared for adult existence

Stunned into surprise
By our own persistent waking
From the sleep that doesn't last

Forever, the endless nothing
We expect to intervene
Between then and now
Between youth and age

Between tonight and tomorrow
The death that will save
Us all from winter's frost

The indignity of Thanksgiving
And New Years, all those new years
That teem as rain

As a chaos of mornings
Unabated, awash in tret and dross
All the things I've kept and lost
The burdens that sustain

Like an Ouroboros devouring
Itself, a circle and cycle
Divining futility

Unfulfilled, unsated
The reckless abandon of hope
Which thrives
Despite my numbered days

Daphne in the Spring

Green tugs like wind
Tension at the fingertip
A twisting sensation
Rubbed against time

Something warm in a place
Frequently cool
A tender *liveness*
That might weep if wounded

Just as bark might peel
Its thickness flung outward
The numb lacework
Stretched around my years

Rain is my balance
In broken soil
Burial or birth
Or both

And the amber gold flow
That is sap
Seeping through delicate limbs
Feels like a pulse

Down into roots
Where there are no words
Only a tight clench
And the tangled surety of place

Part Two
Salt Water

Spell Out a Robin, for Cheer

The robin redbreast
of my Virginia phase
has none of England's robin-red

more like a red-headed youth
like two sisters and a brother
my mother and husband
all of them orange
and none of them urging
Cheer up! Cheer up! Cheer up?
Cheerily!

neither these Virginia birds
the herds of bachelor robins
who all winter long
hold their summer tongues

and I call my Tennessee mother
to tell her how robins
have followed me here

we always worried where they went
when the valley rimed with ice
streams grayed to slush
and the lawn fell silent
deserted by robins
until their return heralded May
here, only their voices migrate

wintering in some riotous place
before thawing in bright demand
to squabble on the fence

breasts flushed with temper
provoking mates to sing
Cheer up! Cheer up! Cheer up?
they're cheerily fat, shiny with rain

and stalk a blindly buried prey
in alert, comedic dance
dashing across the weeds
to wrestle out a feast of worms
busy with the business
of spring's arrival

The Bowerbird's Courtship

Not one is dissatisfied . . . not one is demented
with the mania of owning things . . .
  —Walt Whitman, *Leaves of Grass*

Perhaps the bowerbird feels
Some human desire, some yearning
For the twinkle and sparkle of things

Which can be troved in heaps
To own the eye, to possess
The gaunt imagination

Which sees riches
In a wealth of glimmer
In a shimmer of foil

Tinsel, treasure on equal
With coin and sequin
Silvered mirror sliver

And glass, or paste
All of it costume
Dressing necks and nests

In manic splendor
Spilling over the breast
A riotous sprawl of debris

That fills a powerful need
To collect, to harvest
To hoard a fabulous cache

Of bright, pretty flotsam
To admire and arrange
According to whim

37

And display in clever light
So the weight of things, the splintered
Prism of lust remains concealed

The Tracking

Her cloak hung red and close
Dyed madder rose, alum sealed fiber
Of root and blood, a resinous soak
Before the drape and fold
Before the dread and dawn

Before the wolf came loping
Through shadow and stem, fern
And mold, drawn to the thread
Of scent, scarlet woven girl

With her basket of bread
Her glorious hem and hood
Snarled in thorn, which clung
At her nape, at the warp and weft
Of her bent and perilous path

Unraveled by curious nose
The better to name you with
My dear, my love, my maddening
Rose who weeps in the cold

In the forest reeking of youth
Fresh from rent seams, from dreams
Of wicked tooth seeking what weaves
Through flesh and leaves, the wry and gnarl
Of age that steals, quick quick at her heels

The Fire, Part II

In the house of my marriage we boxed the fire
And stored it in our attic with all the other
Memories, conveniently out of sight
Sealed and secure, metered for efficiency

Squat furnace of piped flame, contained circuit
Of intake, duct, and vent; sensor and fan
Automated exchange of warm tides
That fall from our ceiling and rise again

Out of reach, convection controlled
By an indifferent touch, the brief adjustment
In passing, pause in the hall to add a degree
Or subtract from the thermostat that translates

Comfort as a sliding integer scale scored
In frugal decades, each winter allowed a shade
More reign until we are inured
To the chill, accustomed to this mechanical

Fire that burns in hiding, exiled to the unfinished
Space of school mementos and tax returns
Raw rafters, rolled insulation, and the unused
Hammock we never found time to hang

Turning Forty in a Flood

Where came all this water?
Ripples lapping at my bow
As I wallow in regret
Top-heavy with resent
Unkeeled, heeled heavily starward
Each season my list more apparent

Rudder gone to drift
Ambition to the skies
To constellations, sextant slued
While sails flap in foggy light
Unfurled, lank, unfilled
On my incompetent tack

My complete lack of air
Betrayed by all this froth
By all the depths I plumb
And declare shallow out of spite
No current or tide my ally
No salty catch success

Because I dreamed of land
Of soil and ore, stump and bole
Sweating a noxious milkweed sap
For the monarchs
To lap along their way
Their stolid modern horde

Migrates past my realm
Of algal bloom and silver scale
And silhouettes beneath
That I name fear, with less regard
For leviathan's hunger
Than my mounting thirst
Which aches and burns

Which I cannot quench
Because all this water
It isn't mine to drink
Though it rises to my knees
My thighs, regardless how I bail
And toss it overboard

While I sink in brine
Monarchs strain
And lift gilt wings
Flail in vain, carry on
Without me, without my burden
Of years, heavy from toxin and toil

From the sopping weight of dismay
Angry denial and assorted
Pills I cannot swallow
Because I can't forget, all
This water and guilt
All this blood and learning

All these continents
I'll never reach, never walk
Never reap or sow, never
Settle with enough faith
To trust for spring, to wait
For wind to guide me home

Of Warbler and Quail

Drab little she in the brush
Muttering her song to lure
Someone else

But only I respond
Drawn across the dune
To listen closer

As a child I spoke to quail
I whistled out their *bobwhite* name
To hear them shriek it back

But this little warbler
Outside my beachfront door
Her accent slips my ear

Measures of water wisdom
Refrains of woven nest
Codas that fall silent

Because I have come too near
To understanding
What is lovely on this shore

Of daily tide
Of sandy soil and storms
Of quickening flocks

That speak their sea-swept names
In secret tangled tongues
Of salty sail and oar

And then they fly away
While I struggle, yearn to say
What I remember of briars

Of dry summer streams
And winter dreams
Of silent quail

Hungry among the thistle
Of home, my distant valley home
So many years from here

Poet's Block

An image of a weathered seashell
Keeps my monitor from standing blank
Like a cruel mimic of the blank document
That repels my words
They fall from it
Veer around its margins
Break their brittle syllables against the screen

Which is once more a seashell
I press my ear to the shell's flat shadow
To hear my own intent
The low tidal ebb of phrase
Whispered in computer current
But there is only hum
And static-snap
And the odd warmth of waiting

Nothing whispers from the image
Nothing breathes

And yet all is there
Every conch curve
And shaded whorl
And all my words that failed
To echo the ocean
Or uncover the cloud shrouded sky
Or mention how snails are never simple

Or charge their syllables with metaphor
To mean more than a word
More than a blank screen
More than a poem
I haven't written
Lost for days
In the image of seashell

The Ring

My wedding band doesn't fit anymore.
The ring was cast for a slender,
undernourished extremity, one with young skin
and supple knuckles, one that caressed my lover
in a surfeit of relief, grateful to be wanted
after so many years of knowing myself
unwantable. I loved the idea of being loved
and loved the man who talked
about love as if he alone had solved
its secrets. And the ring was only a symbol.
When I grew and the ring didn't,
I took it off. Maybe if I had invested more,
purchased a few more measures of gold,
maybe then the ring would fit.
But the effort wasn't in me and the money
was needed for other things and it seemed
the start of an endless cycle, constantly
adding to the ring until, in the end,
it would be too heavy to bear.

Undone

This is the house of chores undone
The kingdom of cluttered intent

Where I toil without progress
Up and down the stairs

Through closets and drawers
Of excess, where we hide

What offends the irritable eye
A scrambled profusion of parts

Unused, whether needed or not
In a bookcase or swing

Still here or long gone
From our domestic castle

Of clenched jaw and glare
The turrets of temper

Piled stone upon stone
Mortared with what we didn't do

For each other, or ourselves
With what we didn't discard

In time, simply stored it aside
To stutter free in some later war

All the doors flung open
And cabinets exposed

Spilling the bobbins and bolts
Of our careless disrepair

Underfoot, a bitter shambled state
Of grace, because we stay

To sweep it up again, and say
A house cannot keep us undone

Where I Once Belonged

I am revealed and betrayed
By this mirror truth
About the length of my own leg
Which feels like a child's leg to me
Though I am already wife
Wedded to a new name
And so alien
On my suburban street
With its dearth of empty spaces
And frightening excess of neighbors

Because the lane that is my past
Is lined with weedy ponds
And fields and wooded bogs
And rain
And beats some days
With the rhythm of a hammer
Effortful
Driving nails
To shore up the rotting home
Of my childhood

I often long for dirt
Fresh plowed
Surface cold and damp
From its eternity entombment
Long lumpy furrows
Already ripe
With a harvest
Of turned stones
And cast off secrets
Left by generations before

Such broken maps
Cannot fit together
Will never be seamless
Even if folded
In the same memory
Must be carried in separate hands
That yesterday on my right
And this today on my left
Held whole by a tomorrow
In which it might rain

Adaptable

I've escaped, bolted the house
Driven across town to the park
Where I can be silent, contemplate
The semi-solitude of salt marshes

Not alone because others walk
These trails, those who seek
The same or something different
To each a different kind of peace

In the measured approach of soles
Bicyclists strapped into fancy pedals
A smattering of cameras and party
Of leggy teens, all oblivious to me

As I pause to watch a sunlit raccoon
Forage in an open mire, clever hands
Combing muck for morsels tucked away
Too fast to see what she's eating

And I'm jealous, would almost switch
Pelts for a spell, shed my human trappings
Amble into the unknown and let it devour
My name, my awkward insecurities

My ambitions and failures and calendar
Of expectations, let it teach me new ways
To survive, new rhythms of touch and scent
If only for an hour, let it teach me to live

In the Suburbs, Night Rises

Dew trickles out of grassy lawns
Pours from iris shadows and sighs
In the splash of water spilled
Across a hot driveway

So night begins as a swirl on the ground
As song exhaled from green ponds
Drummed from a deep, wide throat
Of amphibian lust

Which thickens into musk and dusk
To muffle the robin's bright cheer
And damp the cardinal's red aria
Into gray sparrow refrain

While crickets strike sparks in their legs
Raucous wicks in the neighborhood dark
Which might be confused with stars
Or lovesick lightning bugs

This is strange, ember music
Its raspy chorus wild
And its thick, humid rhythm
Calls wild into my past

Where frogs sing down the sun
And insects warn of changes coming
And birds' wings beat
And blood passes to breath passes to bone

       Throbs into sleep
       Where night rises
       Between memory and dream
       Like silence

Part Three
Rain Water

Written Confession

I write therefore I am
Saying the unspeakable
Secrets and sins
Prying open scars

The vaults of forgetting
Excavated and looted
Stolen into memory
No treasure here
Only trespasses

Any explorer would find
My past poorly guarded
Every apology repeating itself

They all mean
I was never innocent

Autumn

After lifeguards and tourists
fold their sandy towels
and flock toward another summer

After thunderstorms and cattle
resume their mutual contemplation
of grass

After bees and wasps and power lines
stop humming
through abandoned afternoons

But before the moon pulls winter
from her deep dark hat of tricks
where it has rocked all summer
between two rabbits
and a molting dove

In those few fleeting breaths
between what we know of life
and what we wish of death

There is a pause
an absence of movement
Everywhere except our lungs

Which cannot help but continue
in and in and out and out
even during the moment of silence

Nature impresses
over her other children
and we hear ourselves
thinking about leaves
while sleep falls over yellow days

Entropy

yarn and ink and memory
looped into patterns
illusions of order

I tie loose ends
trying to finish
scarves and poems

before they unravel
into abstract skeins
tangled, like yesterday

when the past I remembered was not
what anyone else remembered
we were all there together

but we were always flying apart

A Dove, for Beginnings

So today I heard this noise
The one a dove makes in flight
The pitched whiffle of fright

It is, apparently, wings
Sculpted feather beating aloud

Through the neighborhood air
Where all sound begins
With a turbulent leaving

How the dove's wing speaks
Cleaving whistled goodbyes
Into further meanings of flight

Nothing of lung or tongue
Where air is usually sung

I imagine feathers in my mouth
A vocal plumage of facts
A cacophony of acts

Perhaps in every throat, a dove
Yearning toward its mate
Building messy nests of vowel

In which to raise new phonics
To mean more than staying

More than variation's genes
That shaped wings to sing
The mourning dove's departure

In case I wasn't already jealous
Mutely aware of inertia
And fright, and mourning

And the cold silence of hands
With no sounds of their own

To clap against the land, to whiffle
In the wind, to fly away
In search of easier things to say

Doppler Effect

In the last months
I heard grief coming

Unwelcome engine in the distance
Hauling its load of loss ever closer

Louder and louder with each new symptom
Roaring through visits and vigils

Delaying my return ticket to steal more time
Whispering mantras of denial

Panic whining to an unbearable pitch
The pre-dawn call, the respiratory crisis

And failed resuscitation
Everything slipping to shock

As grief's cars hurtle past
Bound for unknown stations

Another Autumn

The garden isn't dying this October
Not like my mother and father died
Decades apart in separate Octobers
The garden's sleep is not eternal

It's only a winter spell, gold leaves spinning
Like hypnotists' watches blurring time
Until gourds droop on brittle vines
And bee balm slumps to the ground

Petunias fade on frail stalks
Mums stop breathing, asters fray
The ginger lilies' nectar fails
Honeysuckle clots in the cold

And I share the yard's exhaustion
Spread blankets of mulch
Anticipating the first frost

A dark, new moon
When the sky will lower
Like a lid as I descend

Into a vault of rumpled quilts
Where dreams wait
Specters of warm relief

Fragmented memories
Welcome regressions
Long, painless hours abed

Listening to the mesmerist's murmur
Tomorrow tomorrow tomorrow
Tomorrow you must wake

And grieve

Finalizing Our Aged Property

The exhausted land reclaimed
Our fence-line
Time blanketed
Obscene barbs
With perfumed honeysuckle

A million twining flowers
With steely resolution
Wrested rusty strands
Toward the soil

A war of decades
Waged on a suspension bridge
Sagging posts and braided wire
Fatigued by the surprising weight
Of so many fragile vines

At last the posts cracked
In surrender
Gave up their substance
To termites and rain

And our boundaries
Crumbled into joyous ruin
Nothing left of fences
To say where we should end
And something else begin

The Cardinals

Two mated cardinals
Muted mother and masked father
Alarmed and flashed around the corner
Through crepe myrtle, plum, and iris

Their single nestling, un-nested
Precocious and half-fledged
Quavered in the awful sun
Exposed, expelled, exploring
The perilous yard

An infant still shaped to shell
Convex and vexed
Voraciously alive
Irresistibly ugly kernel
Of what might be lovely
Clad in summer plume

Though now all hungry gape
Begging nourishment
Little family of fear on the lawn
Watched by the brooding housewife
Who sits her own reluctant nest
Of amniotic memory
Hatching into phrase

And eager to mature
Like the cardinal chick
Which disappeared next morning
Gone from the woodpile and irises
From the bright wing of father
From the red-headed husband
Whose pajama-clad wife
Frets barefoot in the dew

Rescue

Vellum fragile, tense and warm
Two baby rabbits flushed from their nest
Mouse-bodied, with translucent skin
The first I cupped into a glove
And almost couldn't breathe

So much life, contained
Pulsing and hot
Like the blood veined in its ears

Which, though not for owning, I wanted to own
Its immature eyes, its forehead's significant dome
And legs that were meant to flee, even from me
So I returned it to the pine-straw nest
To the huddled sibling rumps

While the second infant fell into a sewer
Into mud and garbage and piled debris
Beneath our dense suburban street

Hours later I snared it free
Hot and muddy and still in the trance
Of overlarge eyes and cowering stance
But cooled by satisfaction, clean in the knowledge
That rabbits should die in the hard-run hunt

Even those nursed in tame bed-roses
Too close to the storm sewer grate
Far from any beagles' noses

Metamorphosis

Nine caterpillars on the milkweed
Monarchs in the making
Nine fairy-tale larvae gnawing
Toxic leaves and stems

One short of a double handful
Gaudy fingers counting happiness
Into September's waning light
In a yard grown wild

With end-of-season neglect
Each vine and flower folding
Its beauty in anticipation
Of fall's many journeys

While a farmer's weed feeds
Next year's flock, fattening heirs
Almost ready for the chrysalis
For the silk unweaving

And flesh reweaving, nine
Marvels maturing toward flight
Toward the necessary leaving
And gathering and leaving again

Of their frail herd, a dwindling
Pulse of butterfly lore paused
In the yard for these brief hours
Nine, eight, seven, six, five

Four, three, two, one last
Sigh of discovery before
I put away the mower
And wave goodbye to summer

Separating the Irises

Knees braced in stinging grass
I learn my own joints
The curve of my spine
A trellis of bone and sinew
Up to collar and throat
Branched into shoulder, then elbow, then wrist
Flowering twin hands full of knuckles

Which dig into the irises
To sort their Gordian Knot
Of root and worm and fungal filament
And cut it from the ground

I am, in this afternoon
A maker of laws against prosperity
Chastising my creation
Which is forever dividing and divining
Kneeling over my raspy flock I prize
Bare a mummified welter of wombs
And begin the violence of separation

Some go back to their beds
Tucked chaste distances apart
Others are cracked from their kin
Exiles bound for foreign lawns

While I linger, remorseful
Among my bruised and scattered irises
Plant knuckles and palms beside the bulbs
Where I feel the whole weight of the Earth
Through my shoulders, my penitent back
Pulling as if I could relent
And pass into soil

To live simply
Unsheltered, in the company of crickets
My womb dividing and divining
Until I am numerous, independent of bone

Coda

Gravity

Water doesn't want
It only weighs

Neither will nor wisdom inform its seep
Downhill, settling to the lowest pool

Rivers cascade and marshes ooze
Toward inlet and gulf
Where tides surge

With the arid moon
Sere face lowered
In serene reflection
Over oblivious blue

Depths that teem with fin and polyp
Oyster clades awash in brine
That neither murmurs nor sighs
Through a shell

Held to the ear we hear
Blood's heave
An eternal chorus
Singing sailors to sea
Dreamers to sleep

Daughters to voice
Their bare feet anchored
In restless churn
On heavy, ancient shores

About the Author

Rae Spencer is a writer and veterinarian who lives in Virginia with her husband and their very spoiled cats. She can be found online at raespencer.com.